W9-ANN-313

DATE DUE

GAYLORD			PRINTED IN U.S.A.

Six Legged World

LIVES OF INSECTS

Lynn M. Stone

The Rourke Book Company, Inc.
Vero Beach, Florida 32964

PHOTO CREDITS
© Lynn M. Stone: cover, p. 6, 8, 11, 15, 19, 20;
© James H Robinson: title page;
© J. H. "Pete" Carmichael: p. 7, 16;
© James P Rowan: p. 12, 13

EDITORIAL SERVICES
Janice L. Smith for Penworthy Learning Systems

Library of Congress Cataloging-in-Publication Data

Stone, Lynn M.
    Lives of insects / Lynn M. Stone.
       p. cm. — (Six legged world)
    ISBN 1-55916-313-5
    1. Insects—Juvenile literature. [1. Insects.] I. Title.

QL467.2 .S789 2000
595.7—dc21

                                        00–036924

Printed in the USA

CONTENTS

LIVES OF INSECTS

You have no doubt met plenty of insects. You've seen them in your house, at your school, and outdoors. Insects can live almost anywhere. A very few even live in icy Antarctica.

Insects are small, six-legged animals without bones. The smallest among them is the fairy fly. It's so small it can walk through a hole in a salt shaker. Even the largest insect, a **species**, or kind, of moth, is only 11 inches (28 centimeters) across.

Insects live almost everywhere, from our houses and backyards to oceans, beaches, forests, and beyond. This damselfly is in a marsh.

Scientists say there are perhaps 10 million species of insects. And in each square mile (2.6 square kilometers) of land there may be billions of insects.

One reason that insects are so plentiful is because of their small size. They can hide easily, and they can live on small amounts of food.

Part of their success, too, is the ability of most insects to fly. Flight helps them escape from enemies and find food quickly.

An insect's small size, wings, and ability to hide help it dodge many animals that would like to eat it.

METAMORPHOSIS

Insects tend to have short lives. However, they make others of their kind easily and often. That ability to **reproduce** helps insects survive in a world full of enemies.

Insects grow to adulthood by going through several different stages, or steps, in life. Different species follow different steps. Most insects follow one of two paths to adulthood.

Both paths are known as **metamorphosis**. That big word basically means to undergo change.

These eggs of a cecropia moth are the first stage of that insect's complete metamorphosis.

The changes during an insect's metamorphosis are often amazing. The whole process can take several days or, in the case of **cicadas**, 17 years!

One type of metamorphosis has three life stages. The other has four. In three-stage, or incomplete, metamorphosis, insects are eggs, then **nymphs**, then adults.

In four-stage, or complete, metamorphosis, insects are eggs, **larvas**, **pupas**, and adults. Most insects go through four stages.

A moth's second stage of metamorphosis is being a caterpillar. This is a saddleback moth's caterpillar.

Larva stage of the scarab beetle is called a grub.
It looks nothing like its adult parents.

Dragonfly nymphs live underwater. As adults, dragonflies may live near water, but not in it.

13

Before insects become adults, most of them look nothing like their adult stage. They may even live in different surroundings. The wingless nymphs of dragonflies, for instance, live underwater.

Insect larvas are wingless and eyeless. Many are legless. They look like worms. Butterfly and moth larvas are known as caterpillars. Housefly larvas are maggots, and beetle larvas are grubs.

When a larva reaches full-size, it quits eating. Then it becomes a pupa.

The third stage of a moth's metamorphosis is the pupa. The polyphemus moth pupa develops in a cocoon wrapping of its silk and leaves.

The best known pupas are those of butterflies and moths. They live in coverings called **cocoons** (moths) or **chrysalises** (butterflies).

Pupas don't eat, but they undergo great body changes. In the pupa stage, a butterfly changes into an adult. When the changes are finished, an adult butterfly crawls out of the chrysalis.

In the final stage of its life, an adult birdwing butterfly crawls from its chrysalis in Malaysia.

ADULT LIVES

An adult insect's main jobs are to feed itself and raise a new family before dying. Some adult insects don't even eat. They live just long enough to mate and lay eggs.

Many adult insects lead short, but fascinating lives. For an insect, life is all business. But people often take pleasure in the working lives of insects.

The "songs" of many insects, for example, may be a summer night's music to people. But the insect noisemakers are hard at work trying to win mates.

Some adult moths, like this Polyphemus, don't eat. They stay alive only long enough to mate and lay eggs.

Insects don't have voices. They make noises by rubbing one part of their body against another. A short-horned grasshopper rubs a hindleg against its forewing. Crickets rub their wings together. Cicadas have built-in "drums" in their abdomens.

All insect sounds have a purpose. A female mosquito's buzzing wing sounds draw the attention of male mosquitoes, for example.

A dragonfly vibrates its wings to warm up before the sun rises on a chilly morning.

BEING COLD-BLOODED

Insects are cold-blooded animals. That means their body temperature is controlled by the air or water temperature around them.

During chilly nights and mornings, insects are cool. They're too cool to stir! In fact, they can't be active until the sun warms them. Some insects help warm themselves by moving their wing muscles rapidly without actually flying.

GLOSSARY

chrysalis (KRIH suh lus) —the pupa and covering, especially of a butterfly

cocoon (kuh KOON) — a moth's pupa and its silk covering

larva (LAHR vuh) — the often wormlike second stage of growth between egg and pupa; a caterpillar, grub, or maggot

metamorphosis (meh tuh MOR fuh sus) — the steps of change that take place in the growth of an insect from egg to adult

nymph (NIMF) — the second stage of growth in many insects, such as dragonflies

pupa (PYOO puh) — the third stage of growth in most insects, between larva and adult

reproduce (ree pruh DOOS) — to make others of the same kind

species (SPEE sheez) — within a group of closely related animals, such as butterflies, one certain type (**monarch** butterfly)

FURTHER READING

Find out more about the lives of insects and insects in general with these helpful books and information sites:

- Everts, Tammy and Kalman, Bobbie. *Bugs and Other Insects.* Crabtree, 1994
- Green, Jen. *Learn About Insects.* Lorenz, 1998
- Parker, Steve. *Insects.* Dorling Kindersley, 1992
- Stone, Lynn M . *What Makes an Insect?* Rourke, 1997

Wonderful World of Insects on-line at www.insect-world.com
Insects on-line at www.letsfindout.com/bug

INDEX